ULTIMATE **MILITARY** MACHINES

BOMBERS

Tim Cooke

A+

Smart Apple Media

This edition published in 2013 by
Smart Apple Media, an imprint of Black Rabbit Books
PO Box 3263, Mankato, MN 56002

www.blackrabbitbooks.com

Brown Bear Books Ltd.
Editorial Director: Lindsey Lowe
Managing Editor: Tim Cooke
Children's Publisher: Anne O'Daly
Picture Manager: Sophie Mortimer
Creative Director: Jeni Child

Library of Congress Cataloging-in-Publication Data

Bombers / edited by Tim Cooke.
     p. cm. -- (Ultimate military machines)
 Includes index.
 Audience: Grades 4-6.
 ISBN 978-1-59920-819-0 (library binding)
 1. Bombers--Juvenile literature. I. Cooke, Tim, 1961-
 UG1242.B6B653 2013
 623.74'63--dc23
                                    2012007410

Printed in the United States of America at Corporate Graphics, North Mankato, Minnesota

Picture Credits

Front Cover: U.S. Airforce

Kfir2001: 29t; MilborneOne: 27t; Robert Hunt Library: 05tr, 07t, 08bl, 10tl, 10cl, 17t, 18, 20, 21t, 21bl, 22, 23tr, 23bl;
U.S. Airforce: 06b, 06cr, 07br, 09t, 10br, 11bl, 12, 14, 15tr, 15b, 16, 17bl, 19tr, 19crb, 19cr, 24b, 25cl, 26, 28, 29b;
U.S. Department of Defense: 04, 08c, 11cr, 13t, 13br, 19crt, 19cl, 24cr, 25bl, 27br; U.S. Navy: 09br; Windmill Books: 05b.

Key: t = top, c =center, b = bottom, l = left, r = right.

All Artworks: Windmill Books.

PO1438
2-2012

9 8 7 6 5 4 3 2 1

CONTENTS

INTRODUCTION

Without warning, bombs rain down from a clear blue sky. The aircraft that delivered the deadly cargo is so high above it can barely be seen or heard. By the time the bombs strike their targets, it is already many miles away. Bombers are some of the most destructive of all military machines.

B-2 SPIRIT

Nonreflective materials

Engines buried in wing

STEALTH BOMBER

The B-2 is designed to attack the enemy undetected. Its thin shape and hidden engines escape most radar detection. It is almost impossible to track.

SPECIFICATIONS
Crew: 2
Length: 69 ft (21 m)
Wingspan: 172 ft (52.4 m)
Max Speed: 630 mph (1,010 km/h)

NONREFLECTIVE: Materials that do not reflect radar signals.

WORLD WAR I

World War I (1914–1918) was the first conflict in which aircraft dropped bombs on a large scale. By 1917, German zeppelin airships and Gotha bombers were dropping bombs on cities, killing civilians. The British also dropped bombs from airplanes on German cities.

WORLD WAR II

In World War II (1939–1945), the Germans used Junkers Ju 87 Stuka dive bombers and long-range Heinkel He111s to bomb enemy cities. The German blitzkrieg conquered most of Europe.

● JU 87 STUKA

▲ Sirens wailing, a Ju 87 Stuka drops its bomb as it dives. The dive bombers struck terror into the hearts of people below.

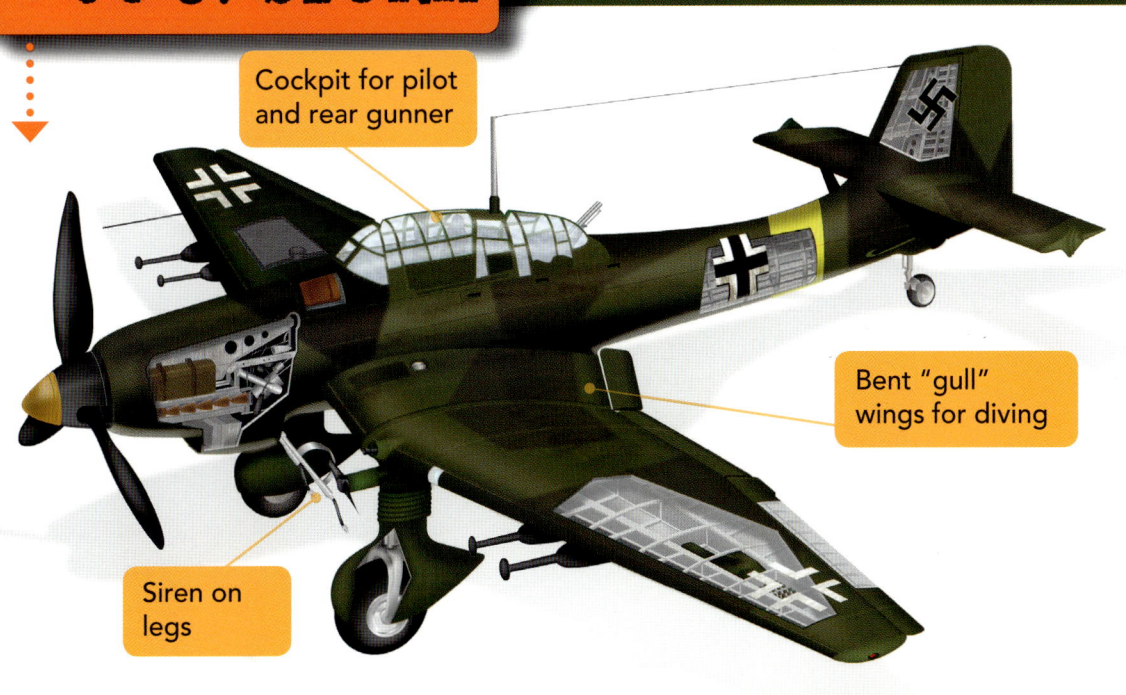

Cockpit for pilot and rear gunner

Bent "gull" wings for diving

Siren on legs

WHAT IS A BOMBER?

A bomber is a warplane designed to carry and drop bombs. Other strike aircraft can also drop bombs, but a bomber has one big difference. It is a long-range aircraft that can hit targets deep in enemy territory. Other attack planes cannot penetrate so deeply.

BOMBS AWAY

A U.S. Air Force B-52 Stratofortress flies over the Pacific Ocean. The B-52 has been in service for 50 years in the U.S. Air Force. It will serve another 30 years before it is finally retired.

● BOEING B-52

▲ A Boeing B-52 carries joint direct attack missiles (JDAM). It can carry up to 70,000 lbs (32,000 kg) of bombs on a single mission.

6

JDAM: A weapons system that converts bombs into guided bombs.

FIRST BOMBERS

The first strategic bombers were multi-engined biplanes. After World War I, they were replaced by all-metal monoplanes. The aircraft were used to bomb urban centers.

▼ The Handley Page V/1500 heavy bomber first flew in 1918. It was four-engine biplane with eight or nine crew.

● PAGE V/1500

F-35 ●

JOINT STRIKE

The F-35 Lightning II was developed as a new fighter for the 21st century. Its experimental form was called the Joint Strike Fighter X-35C.

MONOPLANE: An aircraft with one set of wings; a biplane has two sets.

BOMBER MISSION

A bomber's job is to hit its target on the ground. Today's bombers use different kinds of bombs, missiles, and rockets. Their targets include buildings and bunkers, ships at sea, and troops on the frontline—or even civilians.

◀ Burned-out armor litters a desert road after an Iraqi column was bombed in the 1991 Persian Gulf War.

LONG-RANGE STRIKES

After Japanese fighter planes attacked Pearl Harbor in the Hawaiian Islands on December 7, 1941, the United States joined World War II. As the Allies gained the upper hand, U.S. and British long-range bombers attacked industrial targets in Japan and Germany.

ALLIES: Great Britain, France, the United States, and the Soviet Union.

B-2 DELTA WING

SHAPES AND SIZES

Fixed-wing strike aircraft are different shapes. The delta wing of the B-2 is easy to recognize. Sizes vary, too. Heavier bombers bomb large areas. Smaller strike bombers pinpoint specific targets.

TYPES OF ATTACK

Bombing missions can be either strategic or tactical. Tactical bombings hit smaller targets inside the combat zone. Strategic bombs target an enemy's infrastructure, such as its cities or factories.

SUPER HORNET

▶ A Super Hornet strike aircraft fires a flare over the Mediterranean. Modern types of fighter carry missiles as well as guns.

INFRASTRUCTURE: The basic elements that keep a country running.

NUCLEAR DETERRENT

In August 1945, U.S. bombers dropped atomic bombs on Hiroshima and Nagasaki in Japan. The world entered the nuclear age. New bombers would carry nuclear devices across continents.

◀ Hiroshima lies in ruins the day after the atomic bomb fell on the Japanese city.

LITTLE BOY

The B-29 Superfortress *Enola Gay* dropped the atomic bomb "Little Boy" on Hiroshima on August 6, 1945. Modern nuclear bombs are designed to be launched from submarines.

B-47 STRATOJET

During the 1950s and 1960s, the U.S. Air Force B-47 Stratojet was the most advanced strategic nuclear bomber in the world. It was retired in 1966.

STRATEGIC: Related to the overall aims of a battle, campaign or plan.

FIRST STRIKE

Attacking the enemy before it attacks you is a key job for tactical bombers. They bomb the enemy's fighter aircraft and anti-aircraft artillery. Their job is to establish air superiority. Then other forces can operate more safely.

DESERT STORM

The U.S. Air Force scored early successes in Operation Desert Storm in 1991. It destroyed most Iraqi aircraft fighters before they even took off.

▶ Iraqi planes lie in ruins outside their hangar. A U.S. air strike destroyed them on the ground.

F-117

The F-117 Nighthawk was almost invisible to radar. During the First Gulf War in 1991 it was used to attack Baghdad, the Iraqi capital. It got through the city's defenses to launch night raids.

AIR SUPERIORITY: Control of the airspace above a combat zone.

11

BOMBER FIREPOWER

Bombs are classed as either "dumb" or "smart." Dumb bombs fall freely and explode wherever they land. Smart bombs hit precise targets. They are guided by cameras or by lasers and Global Positioning Systems.

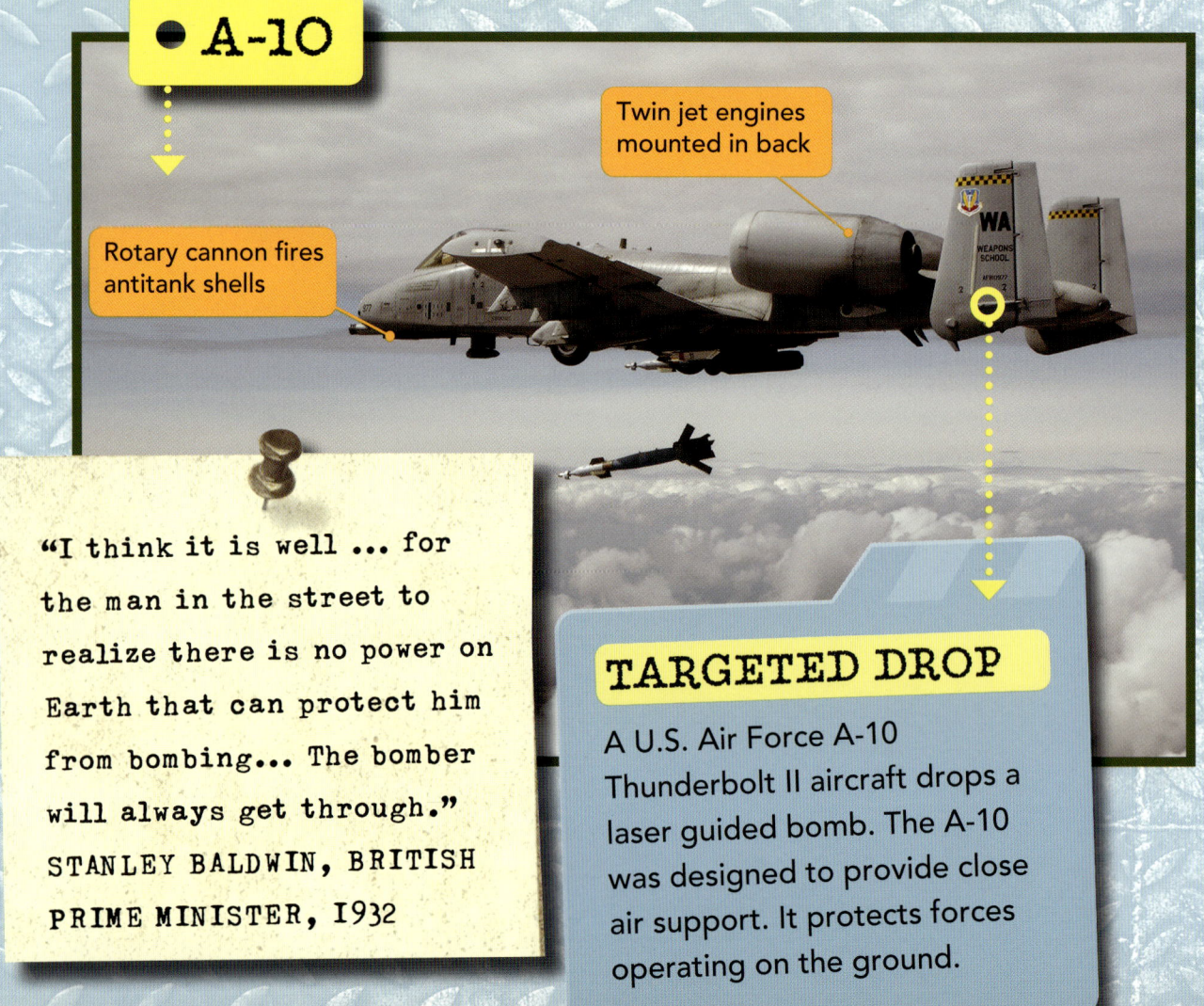

A-10

Twin jet engines mounted in back

Rotary cannon fires antitank shells

"I think it is well ... for the man in the street to realize there is no power on Earth that can protect him from bombing... The bomber will always get through."
STANLEY BALDWIN, BRITISH PRIME MINISTER, 1932

TARGETED DROP

A U.S. Air Force A-10 Thunderbolt II aircraft drops a laser guided bomb. The A-10 was designed to provide close air support. It protects forces operating on the ground.

GPS: A navigation system that uses satellites to find locations on Earth.

DOUGLAS A-1 SKYRAIDER

THE "SPAD"

The Douglas A-1 Skyraider, nicknamed the "Spad," could carry more than its own weight in bombs. It was used in World War II and in Vietnam (1963–1975). It flew low and slow and could often survive hits from enemy fire.

LASER GUIDES

United Nations aircraft used laser-guided bombs to destroy this bridge in Bosnia, in the Balkans. In the 1990s, UN forces intervened in a bitter war in the region.

BOMBS THAT FLY

Bombs are steered precisely to their selected target by being fitted with small wings and guidance sensors. A laser beam is bounced off the target. It provides a path for the bomb's sensors to follow.

LASER BEAM: A thin beam of light produced by a laser.

BUNKER BUSTERS

In 2001, U.S.-led forces went to war against the Taliban in Afghanistan. The enemy hid in caves and tunnels in the Afghan mountains. Conventional bombs could not harm them. U.S. forces used a special bomb designed for underground targets such as bunkers. The BLU-118 fuel-air bomb carries explosives designed to work in underground spaces. The bunker-buster ignites all the oxygen in the air and burns everything in the tunnel.

LOADING UP

OLD WARHORSE

The B-52 has been used in all the major combat zones of the 21st century. During Operation Iraqi Freedom, B-52s fired more than 100 cruise missiles during a single night mission.

▲ Bomb loaders get a B-52 ready for a mission over Afghanistan. The B-52 carries the widest variety of missiles of any bomber.

BUNKER: An underground fortification, often encased in thick concrete.

BOMBER WEAPONS

Modern bombers are expensive, so they have to be flexible. They carry a combination of weapons such as guns, rockets, and missiles, as well as bombs. That means they can be adapted to different functions at a moment's notice.

FIGHTING FALCON

Ground crew prepare an F-16 Fighting Falcon for a mission. The F-16 is a jet that can perform different bombing roles in any kind of weather.

A-10 "WARTHOG"

Pylons under the wings

▲ The A-10 Thunderbolt II is an antitank strike aircraft. It has a cannon and pylons for ordnance.

ORDNANCE: Term for weapons and ammunition.

BOMBER CREW

A large bomber can have as many as fourteen crew members. Every person has a specific task to perform during the mission. In modern strike aircraft, electronics enable a single pilot to fly alone.

STRATOFORTRESS

The B-52 has a crew of five: pilot, copilot, radar navigator, navigator, and electronic warfare officer. There also used to be a tail gunner, but that job is now done by a computer.

"The B-52 gave you a very good ride at altitude, but at low level it was like being hammered. You'd get thrown around in your harness. You'd get knocked around."
CPT WALTER J. BOYNE,
U.S. AIR FORCE

NAVIGATOR: The individual who plots the course of an aircraft.

WWII CREW

WORLD WAR II

The British Short Stirling was a heavy bomber. Its crew of seven was made up of a first and second pilot, flight engineer, bomb aimer/navigator, and three gunners.

SIMULATOR

For bomber crews, simulators are a vital part of training. They can practice maneuvers before flying for real.

▲ This simulator trains the crew to fly the B-2 Spirit, a new generation of stealth bomber.

SIMULATOR: A machine that exactly imitates an activity such as flying.

17

BOMBER TACTICS

The job of a bomber is to get ordnance safely to its target and then to detonate it. Carrying live explosives on an aircraft requires a skilled crew on board—even if it is just the pilot—and technological back-up from the ground.

WATCHING THE GROUND

Early navigators found their way by using maps to identify ground features. That was no use in cloudy weather or at night. Later, they used radar to locate their targets, or even TV images of the ground beneath them.

RADAR: A system that uses radio waves to identify objects.

RECONNAISSANCE

Reconnaissance is a key part of a bomber mission. Spy planes fly at very high altitudes. They use cameras, thermal imaging, and radar to find targets. Satellites also gather information about enemy territory.

▼ The large tail of the Grumman EA-6 Prowler stores electronic spy equipment.

DEFENSES

To defend them from missile attack, strike aircraft carry a radar-detection system. If the system detects a missile, the crew can activate electronic defenses to jam it.

Finding INFORMATION

A mission is only possible if a target has been found. There are various ways to learn about the enemy.

Satellites

U-2 spy plane

Unmanned drone

Bronco observation plane

RECONNAISSANCE: Secretly gathering information about the enemy.

BOMBER HISTORY

Bombers appeared in World War I but had little impact. That soon changed. In the Spanish Civil War (1936–1939) and the Japanese invasion of China in 1937, air raids brought civilians into the frontline.

WORLD WAR II

The Germans began the war with the Blitz, a bombing campaign against Britain. The Allies carpet-bombed German cities, killing many thousands of civilians. U.S. forces crossing the Pacific also brought Japan within bombing range.

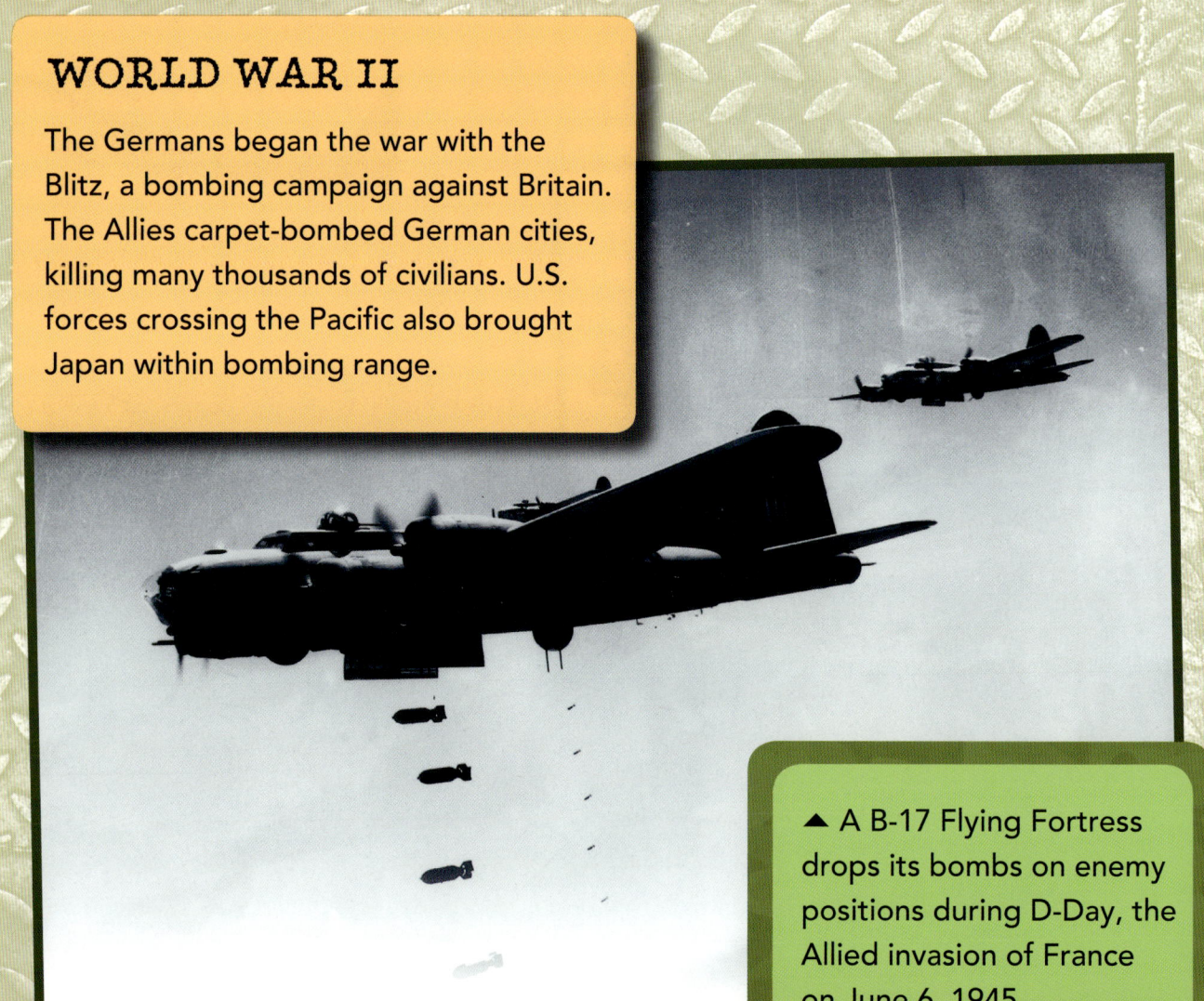

▲ A B-17 Flying Fortress drops its bombs on enemy positions during D-Day, the Allied invasion of France on June 6, 1945.

CARPET BOMBING: To cover a whole area with bombs.

○·······················▶

BOMB RAID

U.S. B-17s fly in formation toward Germany. The Allies bombed enemy cities. They wanted to destroy the morale of the German public so they would stop supporting the war.

NAZI INDUSTRY

Allied precision bombing targeted factories that supported the German war effort. Factories in Schweinfurt made ball-bearings, which were used in military vehicles. The town was bombed twice to shut the factories down.

◀ A ball-bearing factory burns in October 1943 after a bombing raid.

MORALE: The spirit of people, and how positive they feel about things.

DOOLITTLE RAID

When the war in the Pacific began in December 1941, Japan was out of range of U.S. bombers. But in April 1942, 16 long-range B-52s led by James H. Doolittle took off from an aircraft carrier. They flew 500 miles (800 km) across the Pacific Ocean and bombed Tokyo. The Japanese public was astonished. The bombers landed in China and the Soviet Union. Some of the crew were killed or imprisoned, but most survived.

INTO RANGE

A B-25 Mitchell flies above Japan. As U.S. forces captured islands in the Pacific, they built air bases. The bases brought Japan within bombing range.

EYEWITNESS

"The Japanese people had been told they were invulnerabe. An attack... would cause confusion in their minds."

JAMES H. DOOLITTLE

INCENDIARY: A bomb that is designed to start a fire.

TARGET JAPAN

Once Japan was in range, U.S. bombers made frequent raids. In May 1945, B-29s dropped incendiary bombs on the capital, Tokyo. A firestorm began that destroyed the city's wooden buildings. About 100,000 people died.

ATOMIC BOMB

On August 6, 1945, Colonel Paul W. Tibbetts dropped the first atomic bomb on Hiroshima. The bomb instantly destroyed everything within a 10-mile (16-km) radius. About 70,000 people died in the detonation. Many more died later from the effects of radiation.

"The atomic bomb made the prospect of future war unendurable."
J. ROBERT OPPENHEIMER, SCIENTIST, INVENTOR OF THE ATOMIC BOMB

DESTROYED

Only stone buildings survived the bombing of Tokyo and the firestorm it created.

RADIATION: A harmful form of energy given off by radioactive material.

VIETNAM

The Vietnam War (1965–1975) was one of the biggest bombing campaigns in military history. From 1965, U.S. aircraft dropped millions of tons of bombs, rockets, and missiles on targets in North Vietnam, as well as Laos and Cambodia.

▼ A U.S. Skyraider drops a phosphorous bomb on a North Vietnamese target in February 1966.

LINEBACKER II

The Linebacker II offensive was the largest bombing campaign of the Vietnam War. Launched in December 1972, its aim was to force North Vietnam's leaders back to peace talks in Paris.

▼ More than 350 B-52s took part in the night-time bombings of North Vietnam.

PHOSPHOROUS: A chemical that burns the skin on contact.

ENDURING FREEDOM

Operation Enduring Freedom was set up in 2001 to fight Taliban and terrorist forces in Afghanistan. It relied on B-2 Spirits. These stealth bombers entered enemy airspace to drop their bombs without being detected.

"The B-2 ... will help the Air Force gain and hold the ultimate high ground through air dominance during any future conflict."
GENERAL J. JUMPER, U.S. AIR FORCE COMMANDER

B-2 SPIRIT

A U.S. Air Force B-2 Spirit stealth bomber prepares to taxi out of its hangar at Whiteman Air Force Base, Missouri.

◀ Bombers refuel in mid-air on their way to targets in Iraq and Kuwait during Operation Desert Storm in 1991.

GALLERY

Bombers come in different shapes and sizes. They vary from the small one-seater strike aircraft to huge bombers that can carry nuclear as well as conventional bombs.

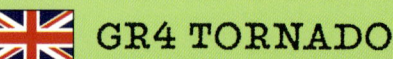 GR4 TORNADO

SPECIFICATIONS
Crew: 2
Length: 54.8 ft (16.7 m)
Wingspan: 45.9 ft (14 m)
Armament: bombs,
   missiles, and guns

The British Tornado GR4 is an all-weather, night and day attack aircraft. As well as firing a large range of weapons such as cruise missiles and smart weapons, it can carry out reconnaissance missions over enemy territory.

CONVENTIONAL: Weapons that are not nuclear.

HAWK T2

SPECIFICATIONS

Crew: 1
Length: 37.5 ft (11.44 m)
Wingspan: 32.6 ft (9.96 m)
Armament: 6,615 lb
(3,000 kg) bomb load, plus
guns and missiles

The single-seat multirole combat aircraft (MRCA) Hawk T2 is the latest version of the Hawk 100 advanced trainer. It is cheaper to build than other aircraft, so is popular with air forces across the world.

A7 CORSAIR II

The Vought A7 Corsair II was used extensively during the Vietnam War. It was an all-weather strike aircraft that could transport heavy loads. It has since been replaced by the F/A-18 Hornet.

SPECIFICATIONS

Crew: 1
Length: 46 ft (14 m)
Wingspan: 38.7 ft (11.8 m)
Armament: 15,000 lb
bomb load

TRAINER: A cheap or out-of-date airplane used to train pilots.

GALLERY

SPECIFICATIONS

Crew: 1
Length: 65.9 ft (20.1 m)
Wingspan: 43.3 ft (13.2 m)
Armament: Nuclear and
   conventional bombs

The F-117 Nighthawk was a twin-engined ground-attack stealth bomber. It was used in Operation Enduring Freedom in 2001 and Operation Iraqi Freedom in 2003 and was retired in 2008.

STEALTH: Uses technology to hide from radar systems.

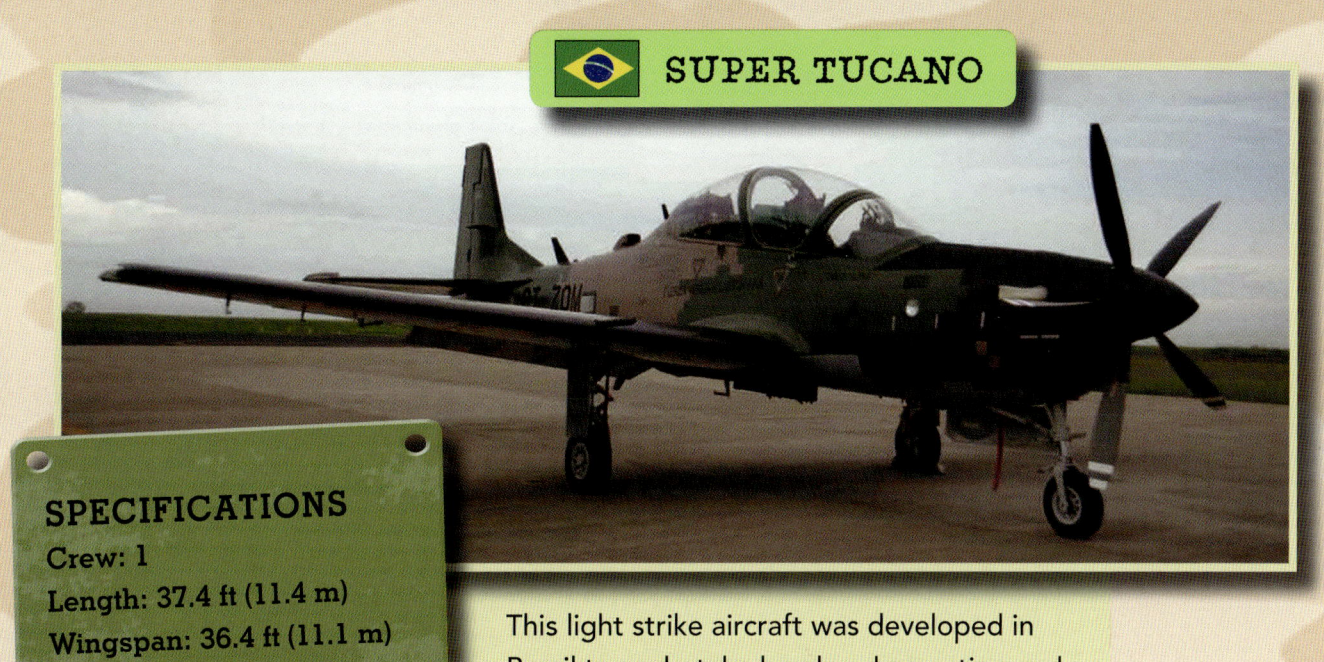

SUPER TUCANO

SPECIFICATIONS
Crew: 1
Length: 37.4 ft (11.4 m)
Wingspan: 36.4 ft (11.1 m)
Armament: guns, missiles, bombs, and rockets

This light strike aircraft was developed in Brazil to undertake border observation and counter-insurgency roles.

F-35

The F-35 is a single-seater, single-engine multirole fighter. It is a descendant of the X-35 of the JSF (Joint Strike Fighter) program.

SPECIFICATIONS
Crew: 1
Length: 51.5 ft (15.7 m)
Wingspan: 35 ft (10.7 m)
Armament: guns, missiles, and bombs.

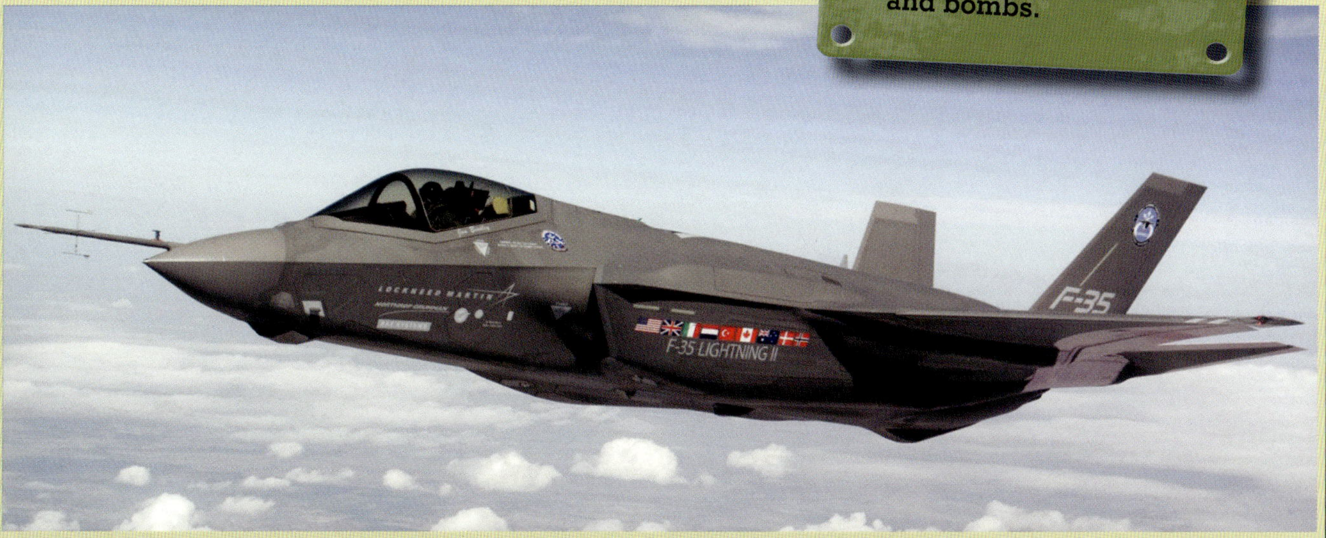

COUNTER-INSURGENCY: Defenses against domestic terrorism.

GLOSSARY

air superiority Control of the airspace above a combat zone.

Allies Great Britain, France, the United States, and the Soviet Union.

blitzkrieg A tactic based on rapid advances with bomber support.

bunker An underground fortification, often encased in thick concrete.

carpet bombing To saturate a whole area with bombs.

conventional Weapons that are not nuclear.

counter-insurgency Defenses against domestic terrorism.

GPS A navigation system that uses satellites to find locations on Earth.

incendiary A bomb that is designed to start a fire.

infrastructure The key elements that keep a country running.

JDAM A weapons system that converts bombs into guided bombs.

laser beam A thin beam of light produced by a laser.

monoplane An aircraft with one set of wings; a biplane has two sets.

morale The spirit of people, and how positive they feel about things.

navigator The individual who plots the course of an aircraft.

nonreflective Materials that do not reflect radar signals.

ordnance Term for weapons and ammunition.

phosphorous A chemical that burns the skin on contact.

radar A system that uses radio waves to identify objects.

radiation A harmful form of energy given off by radioactive material.

reconnaissance Secretly gathering information about the enemy.

simulator A machine that exactly imitates an activity such as flying.

stealth Uses low observance technology.

strategic Related to the overall aims of a campaign or plan.

Taliban An organization that follows an extreme form of Islam.

trainer A cheap or obsolete aircraft used to train pilots.

FURTHER READING

BOOKS

Braulick, Carrie A. *U.S. Air Force Bombers* (Blazers). Capstone Press, 2006.

Green, Michael, and Gladys Green. *Heavy Bombers: The B-52 Stratofortress* (Edge Books). Capstone Press, 2008.

Green, Michael, and Gladys Green. *Long-Range Bombers: The B-1B Lancers.* (Edge Books). Capstone Press, 2008.

Hamilton, John. *B-2 Spirit Stealth Bomber* (Xtreme Military Aircraft). ABDO and Daughters, 2012.

Hansen, Ole Steen. *B-2 Spirit Stealth Bomber* (Cross-Sections: Edge Books). Capstone Press, 2005.

Jackson, Robert. *101 Great Bombers* (101 Greatest Weapons of All Times). Rosen Publishing Group, 2010.

WEBSITES

http://science.howstuffworks.com/stealth-bomber.htm
Howstuffworks guide to the science and development of the B-2 Stealth Bomber.

http://military.discovery.com/technology/vehicles/bombers/bombers-intro.html
Military Channel page listing the Top 10 bombers of all times.

http://militaryfactory.com/aircraft/military-bomber-aircraft.asp
Privately run website with details on more than 175 current and historical bombers.

http://www.historyofwaronline.com/WW2-4.html
Links to pages covering all aspects of air warfare in World War II, including bombers and raids.

INDEX